Did Dinosaurs Eat People?

And Other Questions Kids Have About Dinosaurs

by Donna H. Bowman   Illustrated by Marjorie Dumortier

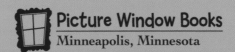

Picture Window Books
Minneapolis, Minnesota

Acknowledgments
This book was produced for Picture Window Books
by Bender Richardson White, U.K.

Illustrations by Marjorie Dumortier
Consultant: M. K. Brett-Surman, Ph.D., Vertebrate Paleontologist

Picture Window Books
151 Good Counsel Drive
P.O. Box 669
Mankato, MN 56002-0669
877-845-8392
www.picturewindowbooks.com

Printed in the United States of America.

 All books published by Picture Window Books are manufactured
with paper containing at least 10 percent post-consumer waste.

Library of Congress Cataloging-in-Publication Data
Bowman, Donna H.
Did dinosaurs eat people? : and other questions kids have about
dinosaurs / by Donna H. Bowman ; illustrated by Marjorie Dumortier.
p. cm.
Includes index.
ISBN 978-1-4048-5527-4 (library binding)
1. Dinosaurs—Juvenile literature. I. Dumortier, Marjorie. II. Title.
QE861.5.B69 2009
567.9—dc22   2009016863

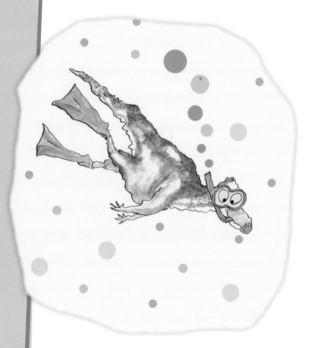

DINOSAURS

Kids have lots of questions about dinosaurs. Were they all big and fierce? How much food did they eat? Could they swim or fly? Were any dinosaurs color blind? In this book, kids get answers.

How long ago did they live?

Paul, age 8

Dinosaurs lived between 245 million and 65 million years ago. Land and seas were in different places than they are today. Human beings did not appear until about 2 million years ago.

Were dinosaurs the first animals alive?

Antonio, age 8

No. Different forms of life came before dinosaurs. These included worms, insects, fish, and trilobites. Trilobites were one of the first creatures to have eyes. Their relatives include today's horseshoe crab.

What were some kinds of dinosaurs?

Nicole, age 8

Were dinosaurs different shapes?

Sara, age 6

The remains of more than 300 different types of dinosaurs have been found. And new kinds are still being discovered. Dinosaurs had many shapes. Ornithomimus, for example, was shaped like an ostrich. Compsognathus was shaped like a large chicken. Triceratops' shape was like that of a rhinoceros.

ORNITHOMIMUS

COMPSOGNATHUS

TRICERATOPS

Where did dinosaurs live?

Joe, age 8

Dinosaurs lived in soggy swamps, rainy forests, and dry deserts all around the world. Some lived on warm seashores. Others lived in very cold places.

6

Could dinosaurs live in water?

Mia, age 8

Could they swim?

Hunter, age 8

No. Dinosaurs did not live in water. But they may have been able to swim a little. For example, Edmontosaurus may have swum across a low river to escape a hungry Tyrannosaurus rex.

How old did dinosaurs live to be?

Justin, age 6

One Tyrannosaurus rex was found to be 25 years old. Scientists believe big plant-eaters such as Brachiosaurus would have taken 75 years to reach full size. Relatives of dinosaurs include modern reptiles. Among these, the giant tortoise can live more than 170 years in captivity.

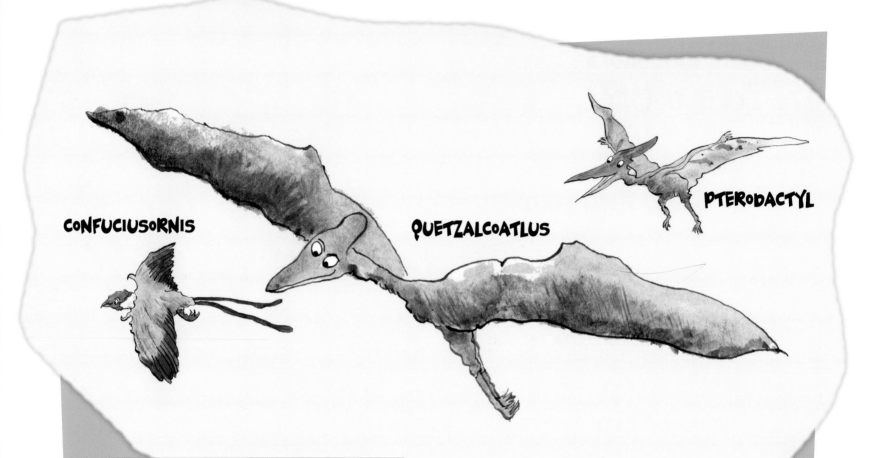

CONFUCIUSORNIS

QUETZALCOATLUS

PTERODACTYL

Were there any birds back then?

Gavin, age 6

Yes. Confuciusornis was one of many ancient birds. It had clawed fingers on its wings. Quetzalcoatlus, a flying reptile, had wings stretching 40 feet (12 meters) across. That's about the length of 10 eight-year-olds lying head to toe!

How many miles could a pterodactyl fly?

Hollister, age 7

One pterodactyl was found 200 miles (320 kilometers) away from a prehistoric shoreline. Pterodactyls were flying reptiles that lived alongside dinosaurs. It is unlikely the pterodactyl swam this far out to sea!

Were dinosaurs reptiles?
Kayla, age 7

How did dinosaurs go to the bathroom?
Partin Elementary School

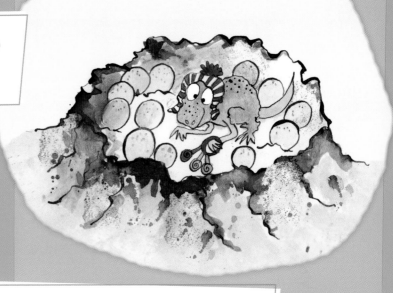

Yes. Dinosaurs were prehistoric reptiles. They went to the bathroom through holes under their tails, like lizards and other reptiles do today. Scientists study dinosaur coprolite (poop that's turned to stone) to see what dinosaurs ate.

How did baby dinosaurs get born?
Browerville Elementary School

What did they look like when they were born?
Sarah, age 8

Mother dinosaurs scooped out a nest in the ground. They laid 10 to 40 eggs and covered them for warmth. Young dinosaurs used a little point on their beaks to break out of their leathery eggshells. Young dinosaurs looked like their parents, only smaller.

What was the biggest dinosaur that ever lived?

Hollister, age 7

The tallest dinosaur was probably Sauroposeidon. This giant stood 60 feet (18 m) tall. That's taller than 10 grown men standing on each other's shoulders! It weighed 60 tons (54 metric tons) and was shaped like a giraffe. The longest dinosaur may have been Argentinosaurus. It was about 150 feet (46 m) long. That's longer than four full-size school buses parked end to end!

What kind of sizes did they come in?
Avery, age 6

How heavy were the dinosaurs?
Niko, age 8

Some dinosaurs were large and heavy. Others were little and light. The heavyweight champ, Argentinosaurus, tipped the scales at 100 tons (90 t). That's heavier than 15 elephants! Little Compsognathus, on the other hand, weighed just 6 pounds (2.7 kilograms)—about the size of a rooster.

Did they have five toes like us?

Kaylee, age 8

Some dinosaurs had five toes on each hind foot. Plant-eaters usually had three to five hind toes. But Compsognathus and other meat-eating dinosaurs had three toes with long claws.

Did some of them have four legs and some two legs?

Christine, age 7

Yes. Diplodocus and other plant-eaters usually walked on four legs. Most meat-eaters, such as Allosaurus, walked on two legs and had two shorter arms.

Did they have big tails?

Matthew, age 8

Some dinosaurs had big tails. But others had small ones. Diplodocus' extra-long tail could harm an attacker. Compsognathus' tiny tail, on the other hand, could barely swat a fly.

Did they all have spikes?

Jordan, age 6

No, not all. Some dinosaurs, such as Ankylosaurus, had bony spikes. But others, like Herrerasaurus, had scaly skin with no spikes. Stegosaurus had boney plates along its back. It also had long spikes on its tail.

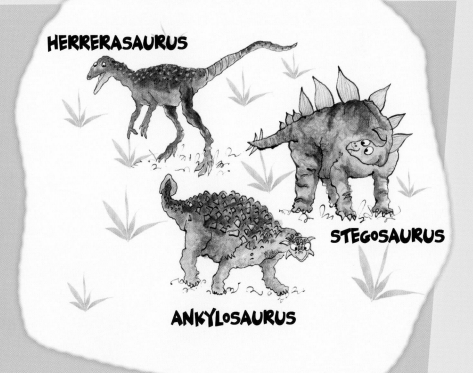

HERRERASAURUS

STEGOSAURUS

ANKYLOSAURUS

How big were dinosaurs' teeth?
Kaylee, age 8

Did they have sharp teeth?
Ethan, age 4

How did dinosaurs wash their teeth?
Sabrina, age 8

Did a dinosaur lose its teeth?
Arianna, age 3

Dinosaurs had different sized teeth. The size depended partly on the size of the dinosaur and what it ate. Tyrannosaurus rex had teeth 7 inches (17.8 cm) long. Hadrosaurs hatched with a beak and hundreds of tiny baby teeth. Dinosaurs didn't brush their teeth. Instead, they drank water to help flush food from their mouths.

Yes. Meat-eaters had sharp teeth. They used them for stabbing and tearing. Plant-eaters had some small sharp teeth used for tearing, and larger flat teeth used for munching on soft plants. And yes, many dinosaurs lost teeth. But they were always growing new ones.

TYRANNOSAURUS REX TOOTH

COMPSOGNATHUS TOOTH

DIPLODOCUS TOOTH

Were dinosaurs color blind?

Jordan, age 8

Probably not. Like today's lizards and birds, dinosaurs may have been brightly colored or patterned. These colors and patterns may have helped dinosaurs find mates or warned others to stay away. Seeing colors would have been helpful to dinosaurs.

Could dinosaurs see at night?

Elaina, age 8

Scientists believe dinosaurs could see at night. However, they used their eyesight mostly during the day. That's when they were most active. During the day, dinosaurs looked for food and mates and watched for enemies.

What did dinosaurs eat and drink?

Luis, age 8

Did dinosaurs eat insects?

Elaina, age 8

Dinosaurs drank water and ate what their bodies were made to eat. Styracosaurus and other plant-eaters ate ferns, leaves, and twigs. Meat-eaters, such as Gorgosaurus, ate the plant-eaters, insects, lizards, birds, and other small animals.

How much food did a dinosaur eat every day?

Chloe, age 7

A lot! Large plant-eating dinosaurs such as Apatosaurus ate 400 pounds (180 kg) of leaves every day! A Tyrannosaurus rex may have eaten a small dinosaur in a day but then not eaten again for a week.

Did dinosaurs eat people?

Cindy, age 8

No. Dinosaurs never ate people. Human beings came along millions of years after all the dinosaurs had died.

Did dinosaurs have brains?

Giselle, age 8

Yes. All dinosaurs had brains. Usually their brains were small, even in large dinosaurs. A 4,000-pound (1,800-kg) Stegosaurus had a brain the size of a walnut!

How did dinosaurs communicate?

Josie, age 8

Dinosaurs likely hissed, roared, or made loud calls. They may have heard each other from several miles away. They may have left scent markings for each other, too.

Did they fight a lot?

Mila, age 6

It's hard to tell if some dinosaurs had a good or bad temper. But dinosaurs likely fought when they needed to. Meat-eaters, such as Giganotosaurus, likely fought for food when hungry. Many plant-eaters lived in herds to stay safe and fought when attacked. Some male dinosaurs may have fought for the attention of females.

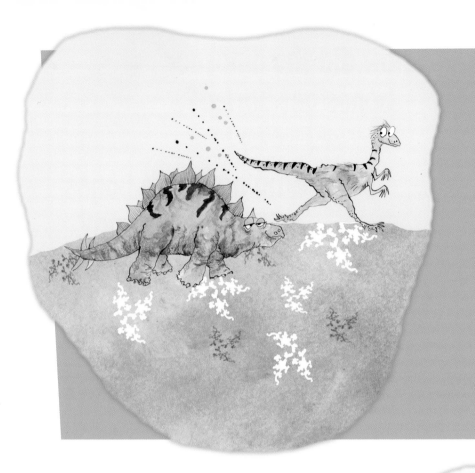

Were all dinosaurs fast?
Cory Elementary School

Not all of them. Meat-eaters, such as Allosaurus, had to be fast to catch prey. Allosaurus could run at speeds of up to 25 miles (40 km) per hour. But large plant-eaters, such as Stegosaurus, were slow. They didn't need to chase food.

How did dinosaurs walk?
Browerville Elementary School

All dinosaurs walked with straight legs. Today's reptiles, such as lizards and crocodiles, walk with bent legs.

What color was dinosaur skin?
Alexandria Elementary School

How did the dinosaur bones get buried?
Browerville Elementary School

Was dinosaur skin rough or smooth?
Alexandria Elementary School

Why are there bones still in the ground?
Hannah, age 7

Colors in skin fossils faded away millions of years ago. Some dinosaurs may have been as brightly colored as today's lizards, snakes, or birds. Others were likely earth colors. Dinosaur skin was probably tough, dry, and bumpy, much like elephant skin.

Landslides, river silt, and desert storms covered the bodies of dead dinosaurs. Over millions of years, the bones and skin became fossils. And then one day, someone found some! Many dinosaur bones have been uncovered around the world. But there are still many, many bones waiting to be found.

20

How did dinosaurs die?

Jasen, age 7

How did the meteorite that hit Earth kill the dinosaurs?

Keith Elementary School

Most scientists think a huge meteorite hit Earth. It caused large volcanoes to blast rock, dust, lava, gas, and ash into the air. This likely blocked sunlight from reaching Earth. The planet then had years of cold darkness. Plants didn't get the sunlight they needed to grow. So the plant-eaters had no plants to eat. Once the plant-eaters died, the meat-eaters had nothing to eat. Without warmth and food, much life on Earth died, including all the dinosaurs.

Is there a dinosaur living today?

Seamus, age 7

No. All dinosaurs died. But their relatives, reptiles and birds, survived. Turkeys, vultures, eagles, crows, crocodiles, lizards, snakes, and turtles are still alive today.

TO LEARN MORE

More Books to Read

Dixon, Dougal. *Agustinia and Other Dinosaurs of Central and South America.* Minneapolis: Picture Window Books, 2007.

Mattern, Joanne. *Allosaurus.* Pleasantville, N.Y.: Gareth Stevens Pub., 2009.

Most, Bernard. *Dinosaur Questions.* Orlando: Red Wagon Books, 2008.

Internet Sites

FactHound offers a safe, fun way to find Internet sites related to this book. All of the sites have been researched by our staff.

Here's all you do:

Visit *www.facthound.com*

FactHound will fetch the best sites for you!

GLOSSARY

captivity—not living in the wild, living under the control of someone else

fossils—the remains of plants or animals that lived long ago

landslide—when loose earth and rock fall down a steep slope

mammal—a warm-blooded animal that has hair and feeds its young milk

meteorite—a rock that falls from space and hits Earth

prehistoric—the time before written history

prey—animals that are hunted and eaten by other animals

reptiles—cold-blooded animals that have backbones and scaly skin; most reptiles lay eggs

silt—tiny pieces of earth on the bottom of lakes and rivers

INDEX

Look for all of the titles in the Kids' Questions series:

Did Dinosaurs Eat People? And Other Questions Kids Have About Dinosaurs
What Is the Moon Made Of? And Other Questions Kids Have About Space
What's Inside a Rattlesnake's Rattle? And Other Questions Kids Have About Snakes
Why Do My Teeth Fall Out? And Other Questions Kids Have About the Human Body